COUNTRY EXPLORERS

CHINA

Janet Riehecky

Lerner Books • London • New York • Minneapolis

First published in the United Kingdom in 2009 by
Lerner Books,
Dalton House,
60 Windsor Avenue,
London SW19 2RR

Website address: www.lernerbooks.co.uk

This edition was updated and edited for UK publication by Discovery Books Ltd.,
Unit 3, 37 Watling Street, Leintwardine, Shropshire SY7 0LW

Words in **bold** type are explained in the glossary on page 46.

British Library Cataloguing in Publication Data

Riehecky, Janet, 1953-
China. - (Country explorers)
1. China - Juvenile literature
I. Title
951'.06

ISBN-13: 978 1 58013 488 0

Printed in Singapore

Table of Contents

Welcome!

We're travelling to China! China is one of the world's largest countries. It lies on the world's biggest **continent** - Asia. Beijing is China's **capital**.

The Pacific Ocean meets China's east coast. Thick forests and more of the Pacific Ocean lie to the south. High **mountains** and dry **deserts** separate China from countries to the north and west.

Beijing is in northern China. About 15 million people call the city home.

RUSSIA

KAZAKHSTAN

Urümqi

KYRGYZSTAN

TARIM BASIN

TAJIKISTAN

TAKLIMAKAN DESERT

AFGHANISTAN   PAKISTAN

PLATEAU OF TIBET

TIBET

NEPAL

Mount Everest

INDIA

RUSSIA

RUSSIA

MONGOLIA

HEILONG RIVER

Harbin

KILOMETRES
0   600
0   500
MILES

GOBI DESERT

GREAT WALL

GREAT WALL

GREAT WALL

NORTH KOREA

Beijing ★

Tianjin

CHINA

HUANG RIVER

YELLOW SEA

TIBET

CHANG RIVER

Chengdu

Nanjing

Shanghai

EAST CHINA SEA

PACIFIC OCEAN

Chongqing

CHANG RIVER

BHUTAN

INDIA

XI RIVER

ZHU RIVER

TAIWAN

MYANMAR

Guangzhou

Hong Kong

VIETNAM

LAOS

THAILAND

SOUTH CHINA SEA

▲ mountains
highlands
deserts
plains
— Great Wall
★ country's capital

Step Up!

China is like a giant staircase. The bottom step lies in the east. This part of China has farmland and rivers.

The middle of China is the second step. This step has mountains, **basins** and **plateaus**.

Rice is a common crop on China's farms.

Western China is the top step. High mountains and cold plateaus lie there. The landscape makes it a difficult place to live.

Map Whiz Quiz

Take a look at the **map** on pages 4 and 5. A map is a drawing or chart of a place. Trace the outline of China onto a sheet of paper. See if you can find the East China Sea. Mark this part of your map with an E for *east*. How about the country of Mongolia? Mark this with an N for *north*. Find the Huang River and the Chang River. Trace these rivers with the colour blue. Next find the Great Wall of China. Colour it red.

The Himalayas are a rugged mountain range in south-west China.

7

Seas and Rivers

Seas touch some of China's shores. The Yellow Sea is in the north-east. The East China Sea is in the east. To the south lies the South China Sea.

Thousands of rivers run through China. The Chang River is the third-longest river in the world. The Huang River is sometimes called the Yellow River because of its colour. Yellow soil turns the river's water yellow!

China's main rivers flow to the east, where the Pacific Ocean lies.

8

Boats, such as this one, carry people across China's seas.

Many people in China travel across the water in boats. People catch and eat the fish that swim in the seas and rivers. Farmers use the rivers to water their crops.

Chinese People

China has the biggest population of any country in the world. More than one billion people live there. Most Chinese people are called **Han**. The Han share **traditions** and a rich **culture**. They speak a language called Mandarin Chinese.

China's city streets are crowded!

Some Chinese people aren't Han. They speak different languages. They have their own traditions too.

The Miao people live in China. These Miao girls are wearing traditional clothing.

Three Is a Family

Many children in China have no brothers or sisters. They might live with just their mums and dads. There are so many people in China that the government made a rule. The rule said that families should have only one child.

One-child families are common in China.

But not all Chinese families have only one child. Some families in the country are allowed to have two children. And Chinese families are not always small. Grandparents, aunts, uncles and cousins make families big. Relatives often live near one another. They might often have get-togethers.

Family Words

Here are the Chinese words for family members.

grandfather	*zufu*
grandmother	*zumu*
father	*fuqin*
mother	*muqin*
uncle	*shushu*
aunt	*ayi*
son	*er.zi*
daughter	*nuer*
older brother	*ge.ge*
younger brother	*de.de*
older sister	*jie.jie*
younger sister	*mei.mei*

This Chinese family is enjoying a meal together.

In the City

Beep! Beep! Chinese cities are noisy places. Millions of people live in Beijing, Shanghai and Tianjin. The roads are jammed with people walking, cycling and driving.

This bustling street is in Hong Kong.

14

Some city residents have houses, but many people live in flats. There are not enough flats to go around. Two families might share one flat.

Tall blocks of flats are common in China's cities.

On the Farm

Many Chinese people live on farms. Some farmers grow rice in wet fields called paddies. Others grow wheat and soya beans.

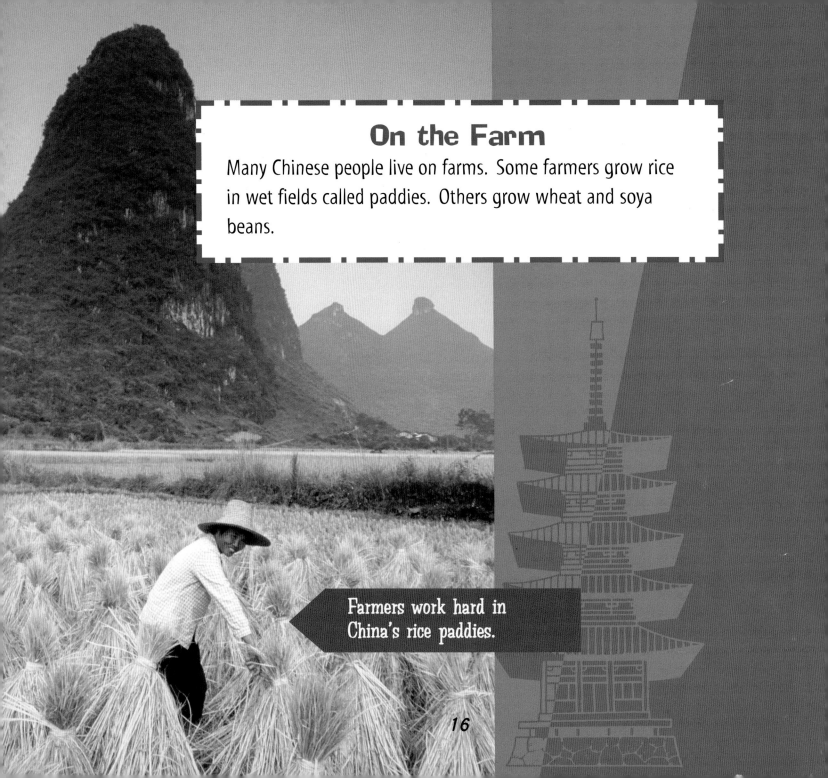

Farmers work hard in China's rice paddies.

Markets in China are often outdoors. This family drove their motorbike to the market!

Farmers sell some of the food they produce to the government. The rest goes to colourful markets.

Getting Around

People in China travel around in many different ways. They drive cars. They ride buses. They also take metro trams and trains. China's city streets are often crowded.

Trams such as this provide an easy way to get from place to place in China.

These cyclists in Shanghai share the road with lots of traffic!

Many Chinese people ride bicycles, but cycling in the city can be hard. Cyclists must share the streets with cars, buses and taxi cabs.

Long Ago in China

Emperors ruled China for four thousand years. The emperors were rich, but most people were poor. In 1911, the Chinese decided not to let emperors rule anymore.

The Great Wall of China is very famous. An emperor started building the wall more than two thousand years ago.

In 1949, a new group took over. They were called the Communist Party. China became known as the People's Republic of China. People called it the PRC for short.

Forbidden City, Beijing

故宫博物院

Dear Uncle Stan,

Today I visited the Forbidden City in Beijing. Long ago, it was the emperor's palace. These days, it is a museum. I saw a gold throne the emperor sat in! Later, I was hungry, so Mum let me buy a roll filled with meat. A girl my age sold it to me from a cart on the street! It was yummy.

Love,
Emmeline

Unc
Anyu

Speaking Chinese

In China, it's not just what you say, it is also how you say it. The Chinese language has four tones. Chinese speakers can change a word's meaning simply by changing the tone of their voice. Here is an example. The word *ma* can mean 'mother' or 'horse'!

Schoolchildren laugh and talk with one another. Do you think they're speaking Chinese?

China's schools teach students to speak one form of the Chinese language.

People in different parts of China speak Chinese in different ways. In schools across China, children learn to speak the same kind of Chinese. That way, people all over the country can use the same language to talk to one another.

What a Character!

Chinese does not have an alphabet. Instead, a symbol called a **character** stands for each word. There are many characters. Learning to write can be hard work!

Children must practise for many years to learn to write correctly.

24

Drawing characters is a form of art in China. Writers use special brushes and black ink. They copy the characters onto white sheets of paper.

This Chinese character means 'love'.

25

Religion and Respect

Children in China respect older people. The Chinese believe that older people are wise. Young people ask their grandparents for advice when times are confusing.

Chinese grandparents share their knowledge with younger family members.

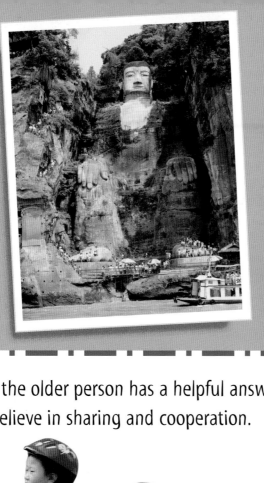

The Biggest Buddha

Some people in China believe in the Buddha's teachings. The Buddha was a religious leader. He lived long ago. The world's biggest statue of the Buddha is carved in the side of a cliff in China. It took workers about one hundred years to carve. Two people can sit side by side on one of the statue's toenails!

Often the older person has a helpful answer. Chinese people also believe in sharing and cooperation.

Cooperation is an important value in China. Schoolchildren learn to work and play together.

Happy New Year!

Chinese New Year is a special festival. Everyone wants the new year to have a happy start. A huge party takes place. The party lasts for fifteen days.

Children get red envelopes on Chinese New Year. The envelopes have gifts of money inside.

Parades fill the streets. People make giant puppets dance. A lion puppet at the beginning of the parade scares away bad spirits. A long paper dragon puppet ends the parade.

Water Dragon

Why does a dragon puppet end the parade? In Chinese stories, dragons are not scary. They are wise and helpful. They bring people water to help crops grow. So in China, a dragon puppet brings good luck at the end of a parade.

A dragon lantern brightens a Chinese New Year celebration.

School Days

Reading, writing and arithmetic - that's what Chinese students study. Does that sound like what you learn about in school?

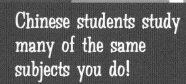

Chinese students study many of the same subjects you do!

These students are from Shanghai.

Children in China go to primary school, just like children in the United Kingdom. Many Chinese teenagers stay at school and then go on to college, but some get jobs instead.

Story Time
The Chinese tell many stories. Some are about adventures. Others are long poems or **folk tales**. Some stories are new. Others are very old.

This picture shows a scene from *The Romance of the Three Kingdoms*, a famous Chinese story.

Folk tales that teach lessons are popular. These stories might be about sharing. They might be about helping others.

A young boy in traditional clothing reads about Chinese culture. Folk tales are an important part of China's culture.

'The Magic Goldfish'

Once upon a time, there lived a young woman named Ye Shen. Ye Shen had a wicked stepmother. The stepmother killed Ye Shen's pet goldfish. Ye Shen was sad. She kept the fish's bones to remind her of her pet.

One day, everyone in town went to a festival. Ye Shen had to stay home. She had no nice clothes to wear. But then something amazing happened. The fish bones saved the day! They turned out to be magical. They gave Ye Shen beautiful clothes. Ye Shen went to the festival. At the party, a king fell in love with her. But Ye Shen left before the king learned her name. She also left something behind - her shoe! Can you guess how the story ends? Hint: Think of Cinderella.

Clothes

People in China wear all different kinds of clothes. Lots of people choose comfortable shirts or trousers. Their clothes probably look a lot like the clothes you wear.

Comfortable clothes are a popular choice in China.

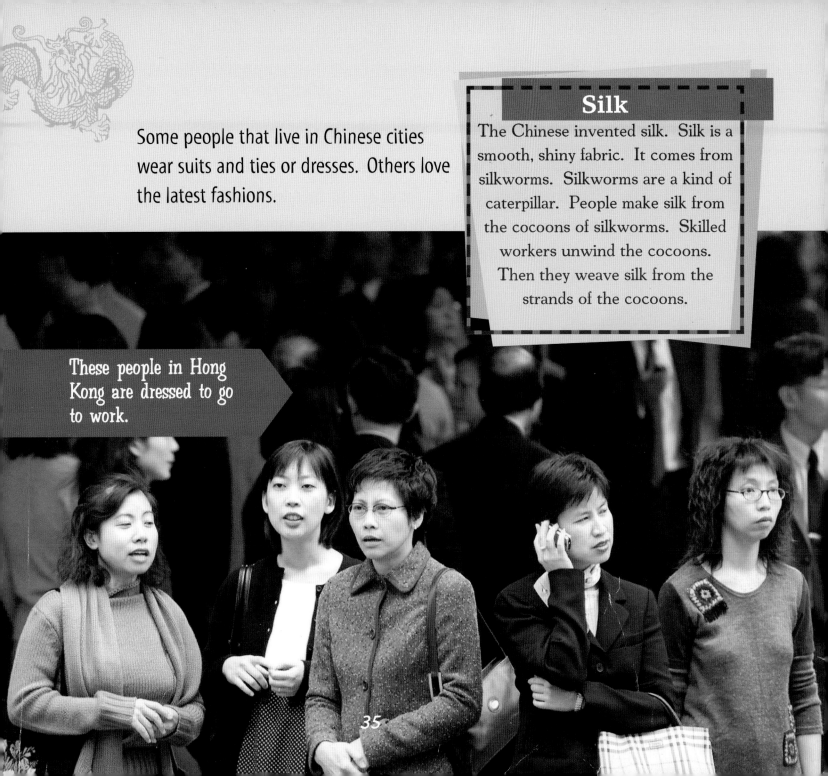

Some people that live in Chinese cities wear suits and ties or dresses. Others love the latest fashions.

Silk

The Chinese invented silk. Silk is a smooth, shiny fabric. It comes from silkworms. Silkworms are a kind of caterpillar. People make silk from the cocoons of silkworms. Skilled workers unwind the cocoons. Then they weave silk from the strands of the cocoons.

These people in Hong Kong are dressed to go to work.

Playtime

Martial arts are popular in China. Martial arts are a type of exercise. They are also a form of self-defence. Some people practise martial arts each morning. They meet in parks and exercise together.

Young martial arts students enjoy their classes.

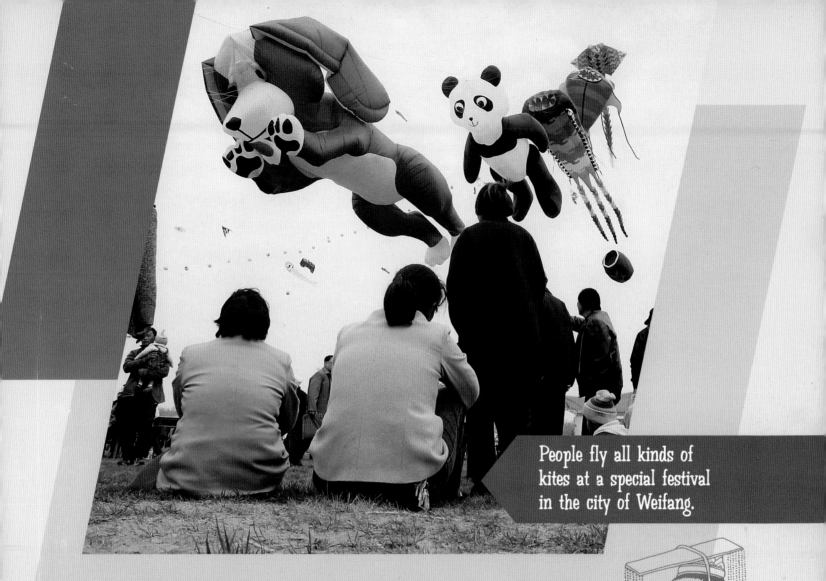

People fly all kinds of kites at a special festival in the city of Weifang.

Children in China love to fly kites. Table tennis is popular too. Gymnastics is a popular sport. Many Chinese gymnasts have gone to the Olympic Games.

Doctors

Can sticking needles in your skin cure a headache? A Chinese doctor might think so! This practice is called acupuncture. The Chinese believe acupuncture can cure more than one hundred diseases. But do not try this at home! Only experts know how to do acupuncture correctly.

Chinese doctors use acupuncture to help patients feel better.

Acupuncture is a traditional cure in China. Not all Chinese doctors use acupuncture. Many give out pills and use modern tools instead. Some doctors use both modern and traditional methods.

Many doctors in China use modern methods to treat patients.

Fruit is for sale at this outdoor market.

Shopping for Food

Many Chinese people shop at outdoor markets. There they buy fresh foods to eat. They often spend lots of time looking for the best prices.

People in China eat many different foods. In the south, farmers grow a lot of rice. People who live nearby eat rice at almost every meal. In the north, wheat is a major crop. People there make wheat into noodles. Cooked vegetables are important parts of meals across China.

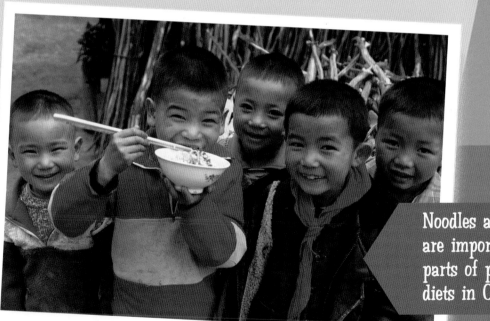

Noodles and rice are important parts of people's diets in China.

Mealtime!

Yummy stir-fries are popular in China. First, a cook chops meat and vegetables into bite-size pieces. The next step is frying the food over a hot fire.

A chef prepares a meal outdoors in Beijing.

Eating With Chopsticks

If you ate a meal in China, you probably would not use a knife and fork. Instead, you might use chopsticks! Chopsticks are long, thin sticks. People hold them in one hand. Experts use them like a pair of fingers. It can take a long time to learn to use chopsticks well.

The cook stirs the food in a pan called a wok. Stirring stops the food burning while it fries.

Stir-fried vegetables are crunchy and delicious!

THE FLAG OF CHINA

China's flag is red and yellow. Five yellow stars sit in the upper left-hand corner of the solid red flag. Red is an important colour in China. The Chinese people often use red in festivals. Red also stands for the Communist Party. People have different ideas about what the yellow stars stand for. Some say they stand for the People's Republic of China. Others say they stand for China's ethnic groups, while others think the stars stand for unity. China's citizens are unified in the People's Republic of China.

FAST FACTS

FULL COUNTRY NAME: People's Republic of China

AREA: 9.6 million square kilometres (3.7 million square miles) or about the same size as the United States

OFFICIAL LANGUAGE: Mandarin Chinese

POPULATION: about 1,313,973,713 (1.3 billion)

CAPITAL CITY: Beijing

MAIN LANDFORMS:

MOUNTAINS: Himalayas, Kunlun, Pamirs and Tian Shan

DESERTS: Gobi, Mu Us and Taklimakan

PLATEAUS: The Plateau of Tibet

RIVERS: Huang, Chang, Xi, Heilong, Li

ANIMALS AND THEIR HABITATS:

DESERT: Bactrian camels

RIVERS: Chinese alligators, Chinese river dolphins

FOREST: giant pandas

GLOSSARY

basin: a hollow place in the land, often with a lake at the bottom. Basins are near mountain ranges.

capital: a city where the government is located

character: a picture or symbol that stands for a whole word or for a word sound

continent: any one of seven large areas of land. The continents are Africa, Antarctica, Asia, Australia, Europe, North America and South America.

culture: the way of life, ideas and customs of a particular group of people

desert: a dry, sandy or rocky region

folk tale: a story told by word of mouth from grandparent to parent to child. Many folk tales are written down in books.

Han: the name of the biggest group of Chinese people

map: a drawing or chart showing all or part of the Earth.

martial arts: a type of exercise and a form of self-defence. Martial arts include judo, kendo, aikido and karate.

mountain: a part of the Earth's surface that rises high into the sky

plateau: a large area of high, level land

tradition: a custom, belief or practice that people in a particular culture pass on to one another

TO LEARN MORE

BOOKS

Jenner, Caryn. *Welcome to China* (DK Readers) DK Publishing (Dorling Kindersley), 2008.

Parker, Vicky. *China* (Young Explorer: We're From) Heinemann Library, 2006.

Roop, Peter and Connie Roop. *A Visit To: China* Heinemann Library, 2008.

Shuter, Jane. *Ancient Chinese* (History Opens Windows) Heinemann Library, 2006.

WEBSITES

The British Museum: Ancient China
http://www.ancientchina.co.uk/menu
.html
This website from the British Museum includes information on Chinese writing, arts, crafts, history, geography and more.

China
http://www.timeforkids.com/TFK/hh/
goplaces/main/0,20344,536982,00.html
On this fun site from *Time for Kids,* you can take a virtual tour of China, learn common Chinese phrases and send a postcard to a friend.

INDEX

The photographs in this book are used with the permission of: © China Photos/Getty Images, pp 4, 9, 27 (bottom); © age fotostock/SuperStock, pp 6, 8, 16, 43; © Jon Arnold Images/SuperStock, p 7; © Bob Krist/Corbis, pp 10, 36; © Robin Smith/Art Directors, p 11; © Yang Liu/Corbis, p 12; © Reed Kaestner/Corbis, p 13; © Viviane Moos/Corbis, p 14; © Mark Ralston/AFP/Getty Images, pp 15, 17; © Nick & Janet Wiseman/Art Directors, p 18; © Neil Ray/Art Directors, p 19; © Guang Niu/Getty Images, pp 20, 37; © Yoshio Tomii/SuperStock, p 21; © Cory Langley, pp 22, 26, 34; © Michael Prince/Corbis, pp 23, 30; © Randy Faris/Corbis, p 24; © Gareth Brown/Corbis, p 25; © Hidekazu Nishibata/SuperStock, p 27 (top); © Franklin Lau/Corbis, p 28; © Bohemian Nomad Picturemakers/Corbis, p 29; © Tibor Bognar/Art Directors, p 31; © Asian Art & Archaeology, Inc./Corbis, p 32; © Hu Weiming/ChinaFotoPress/Getty Images, p 33; © FREDERIC J. BROWN/AFP/Getty Images, p 35; © Lisette Le Bon/SuperStock, p 38; © GOH CHAI HIN/AFP/Getty Images, p 39; © Robert Belbin/Art Directors, p 40; © Liu Liqun/Corbis, p 41; © STEPHEN SHAVER/AFP/Getty Images, p 42. Illustrations by © Bill Hauser/Independent Picture Service.
Cover: © ChinaFotoPress/ZUMA Press.

This book was first published in the United States of America in 2008.